JOSEPH WALLACE

authorHOUSE®

AuthorHouse™ UK
1663 Liberty Drive
Bloomington, IN 47403 USA
www.authorhouse.co.uk
Phone: 0800.197.4150

Published by AuthorHouse 08/09/2016

ISBN: 978-1-5246-6207-3 (sc)
ISBN: 978-1-5246-6206-6 (e)

Print information available on the last page.

This book is printed on acid-free paper.

Scripture quotations marked NKJV are taken from the
New King James Version. Copyright © 1982 by Thomas
Nelson, Inc. Used by permission. All rights reserved.

INTRODUCTION

Blessing is a special gift that God bestows upon His children. People who are blessed are blessed in everything in their life, including health (John 3:2). They are guaranteed for heaven (Mal. 3:10); they will flourish as a palm tree (Ps. 92:12); their blessings will be above all people (Deut. 7:14); their soil will be blessed (Deut. 28:4). They shall be spotted out as blessed persons when they are with friends or family members. They will be the head and not the tail. The Lord will bless everything they do (Deut. 28:6).

When God blesses you, He takes you as recognising Him as your source of strength. You may reach a certain height in life or achieve a certain position, and as a blessed person you must acknowledge that your success and achievement come from God and not from your own might (Deut. 8:17–18). It is God who teaches you to profit, who leads you to the way you should go (Isa. 48:17). As long as you seek God, He will make you prosper (2 Chr. 26:5).

The word of God states that you must seek the Kingdom of God first, and all other things shall be added unto you (Matt. 6:33). Your service to God must be paramount (Job 36:11); you must always obey God's commandments (1 Kgs. 2:3–4). The fear of God must always be in your heart. As it is written in Psalm 112:1–3:

> Praise the Lord! Blessed is the man who fears the Lord, who delights greatly in His Commandments, His descendants will be mighty on earth, the generation of the upright will be blessed. Wealth and riches will be in his house, and his righteousness endures forever.

Sin destroys the manifestation of your blessings from God. It is therefore better to confess your sins and seek total repentance; when you do, you will have the mercy of God (Prov. 28:13). Be prayerful, as the word of God says to a believer that whatever things you ask for in prayer, believing, you will receive (Matt. 21:22). If you want God's blessings, do not cheat anybody who deals with you in your life. Cheating is abominable in the sight of God (Deut. 25:13–16).

It is very important that those who need the blessings of God cultivate the habit of giving. Those who give freely from the heart to support the work of God, sharing part of what God has given to them, reap abundance from what they sow. Those who seek the blessing of God must constantly use the prayers I will share here.

These prayers may be used any time. Pray in absolute confidence in your room alone, standing. Lock the doors and concentrate on the contents of these prayers, because you are standing in front of the Holy Spirit who is eager to take your prayers to God for your spiritual or physical breakthrough, where your name is already written in the book of the blessed people. God's response will be immediate, but where you particularly require a quick response, pray with fasting from six in the morning until six in the evening, continuously, for three days.

Start the following prayers by singing songs of praise in your room for five or ten minutes. Please note that you are standing before God. Humble yourself, as God is ready to listen to your prayers.

—J. Wallace

THE
PRAYERS

Thank the Father

Lord God Almighty, my father in Heaven, I thank You for what You have done in my life. I know You have blessed me, and I believe You continue to bless me and my household. Any sin I have committed in my life which stands as a hindrance in my life, Lord, my father, forgive me. *Amen*.

Thank God

In the glorious name of my Lord, Jesus Christ of Nazareth. Father in heaven, I thank You most sincerely for lifting Your mighty hand to protect me from the grip of demonic powers, just as You protected the Israelites from Pharaoh. Lord, as You were the banner for the Israelites, continue to be my banner in Jesus's name. I thank You for continuing to be commander of my soul against any evil forces fighting me. I thank You furthermore for giving me victory over Satan through our Lord Jesus Christ. *Amen.*

Once Blessed, Always Blessed

In the mighty name of my Lord Jesus Christ of Nazareth. My father in heaven, when You bless somebody, nobody can take the blessing from that person if the person is by faith Your believer. Your word says, "Let them curse, but you will bless" (Ps. 102:28a). Your word says further that Your eye is on all Your blessed children like me. I stand by faith in the Lord Jesus Christ to command that no demonic or evil forces, principalities, or powers can take my blessings from me. In Jesus's mighty name, I command the Holy Spirit and the mighty angels of the Lord to guard me always, as I am the blessed child of God. *Amen.*

I Claim My Blessings

In the Blessed Name of My Lord Jesus Christof Nazareth, my Father in Heaven, You are seated at the right hand of God on my behalf as my attorney against any false accusation against me for my sins. You protect my blessings. When the accuser opens his mouth wide to falsely accuse me because he wants to take my blessings from me and sell them to another person, I declare by the mighty name of my Lord Jesus Christ that any accuser or principality making any attempt to destabilise or delay the manifestation of my blessings from God will be slapped in the face by the Holy Spirit. This shall come to pass in Jesus's mighty name. The light of God shall continue to shine on my way (Job 22:28). I believe that whatever I have requested in this, my prayer, I have received it. *In Jesus's mighty name, amen.*

Your Word Builds My Confidence for Blessing

In the mighty name of my Lord Jesus Christ of Nazareth. Father in heaven, Your word says that anybody who recites Your word always in his heart You will bless to the extent that nobody can challenge him (Josh. 1:8). Lord, I wake up every morning with Your word (Ps. 5:3). You lead me out in Your righteousness in my daily work because I know that my help for the day's work comes from You who is my Lord who made heaven and earth. Who then can challenge my blessing from You, Lord, as I am Your promising child and the great-great-grandchild of Abraham? Nobody can seize my blessings from You. *Amen.*

Lord, Bless Me in All Things

In the mighty name of my Lord Jesus Christ of Nazareth. God of Grace, it is written in Mark 11:23: "For assuredly, I say to you, whoever says to this mountain, 'Be removed, and be cast into the sea' and does not doubt his heart but believes that those things will be done, he will have whatever he says." Bless me in all things I lay my hand on, just as You blessed Abraham in Genesis 24:1, saying "Now Abraham was old, well advanced in age; and the Lord had blessed Abraham in all things." Lord, bless me in all things, just as you have blessed Abraham, because by faith he is my great-great-grandfather, and I am the rightful successor in title of the blessings You endowed on him. *Amen.*

God Bless Me to Be Fruitful

In the blessed name of my Lord Jesus Christ of Nazareth. My heavenly father, when my great-great-grandparents (Adam and Eve) were created, God blessed them and said, "Be fruitful and multiply; fill the earth and subdue it" (Gen. 1:28). By faith I inherit that blessing and promise to be fruitful as it has come from You. Lord, this, Your blessing, will enable me to walk worthy of Your praise by advancing in Your word. Lord God Almighty, continue to bless me to be fruitful as You have promised. *In Jesus's mighty name, amen.*

In Genesis 1:28, it is written, "Have dominion over the fish of the sea, over the birds of the air, and over every living thing that moves on earth." Lord God Almighty, thank You for giving me dominion over every living thing that moves on the earth. Lord, thank You for Your abundant blessing which I cannot buy with money but have been given by Your grace. *Amen.*

Lord God Almighty, what comes from Your mouth cannot be challenged. You said to Abraham in Genesis 17:20, "And as for Ishmael, I have heard you. Behold I have blessed him, and will make him fruitful, and will multiply him exceedingly. He shall beget twelve princes, and I will make him a great nation." Lord God Almighty, continue to bless me to be fruitful and to be the envy of my enemies. *In Jesus's name, Amen.*

I Have Been Blessed from the Beginning

In the precious name of my Lord Jesus Christ of Nazareth. Almighty Father, Your word says that when You bless somebody, the blessing extends to all his family. I understand this to mean that all the family members of Your blessed child stand blessed; it is written in Genesis 9:1, "So God blessed Noah and his sons, and said to them 'Be fruitful and Multiply and fill the earth.'" Lord, Noah is the great-grandson of Adam and Eve. Your blessing to Adam and Eve has extended to Noah, and by faith I claim that blessing as well for myself and my family. I am a blessed child of God by succession. From now on, I stand blessed, and I will continue to be fruitful and multiply to the annoyance of my enemies and to the glory of God Almighty. *In Jesus's name, amen.*

I Stand Blessed on Everything

In the blessed name of my Lord Jesus Christ of Nazareth. I boldly say to all my enemies that whether they like it or not, I stand blessed by God in everything. This is God's providence on my life. In Genesis 24:1, it is written: "Now Abraham was old, well advanced in age and the Lord had blessed Abraham in all things." Lord, as You have promised, bless me in everything. *In Jesus's name, amen.*

I now stand here and ask my enemies to answer me that if God has blessed me on everything as His word says, who is that enemy who says that he will disturb my blessing? If the word of God says that God is with me, who can be against me? *Nobody.* God was with David, and nobody could challenge him. David wrote in Psalm 18:2: "The Lord is my rock and my fortress and my deliverer, My God, My strength, in whom I will trust; My shield and the horn of my salvation, my stronghold." Any blessing and strength David needed, God gave it to him. Lord God Almighty, bless me and give me strength as You gave to David to conquer his enemies for Your children in Israel. *Amen.*

I Am Blessed as a Descendant of Abraham

In the blessed name of my Lord Jesus Christ of Nazareth. My father in heaven, Your word says that when You bless somebody, the blessings pass on to the following generations of the person originally blessed. Hence, Your blessing to Abraham (Gen. 12:3) passed on to Isaac (Gen. 25:5, 26:12) and to Ishmael (Gen. 17:20). Laban was blessed (Gen. 30:32), Jacob was blessed (Gen. 32:29; 35:9), and Joseph was blessed (Gen. 41:39–44). When a blessed person enters your house, your household becomes blessed, just as Potiphar's household was blessed because the blessed Joseph was in the house. It is written in Genesis 39:5, "so it was from the time that he had made him overseer of his house and all that he had that the Lord blessed the Egyptian's house for Joseph's sake, and the blessing of the Lord was on all that he had in the house and in the field." Lord, let the blessings on me pass on to all my descendants as You did to Potiphar's household. *In Jesus's mighty name, amen.*

I Lack Nothing Because of My Blessing

In the merciful name of my Lord Jesus Christ of Nazareth. You do not win war for Your people because of the number of soldiers they go to war with; neither do You bless people because of their numbers. Israel is the very least people in the world from the time past and today, but as you have blessed Israel, they lack nothing, not even in the wilderness. It is written in Deuteronomy 2:7, "For the Lord your God has blessed you in all the work of your hand. He knows your trudging through this great wilderness. These forty years the Lord your God has been with you; you have lacked nothing." Lord, bless me as You have blessed Israel, so that I will lack nothing. Everything will be in abundance in my life. *In Jesus's name, amen.*

All Blessings Belong to God

Lord God Almighty, King of Kings, Alpha and Omega, when You lift up Your hand, nobody can put it down. When You put Your hand down, nobody can lift it up. You bless anybody like myself You want to bless. Lord, put me in Your good books of blessings so that I can be the envy of my enemies, just as David was the envy of Saul. It is written in 2 Samuel 5:10: "So David went on and became great, and the Lord God of hosts was with him." Lord, as You were with David, be with me always. *In Jesus's name, amen.*

Lord, I am proud to enjoy Your blessings. Lord, bless me to have a long healthy life as You blessed Methuselah. *In Jesus's name, amen.*

I Capture My Blessings as a Billionaire in Your Word

In the mighty name of my Lord Jesus Christ of Nazareth. My heavenly father, I need Your blessings to be a spiritual billionaire in Your word. That blessing must be accompanied by righteousness, fruitfulness, and obedience to Your word, to seek Your kingdom first. Lord, I am not asking too much, because Your word says that whatever I ask in Your name, I will receive (John 14:14; Job 22:28). By faith in your word, I am boldly asking for Your blessings in righteousness, abundance, fruitfulness, and health. *Amen.*

I Am a Blessed Child

In the truthful name of my Lord Jesus Christ of Nazareth. Your word says that blessed are those who do not take the advice of those who do wrong but live on Your word. I stand before You and state that I was born by You and as such must abide by Your word. Your word assures me that as a descendant of Abraham, I am blessed. Lord, You have promised my great-great-grandfather Abraham that You will keep Your promise of blessing to him and his descendants, which include me. You will be his God and the God of his descendants (Gen. 17:7). Lord God Almighty, I stand before You in the name of my Lord Jesus Christ and accept Your blessings on me and all my descendants. *In Jesus's mighty name, amen.*

Light on My Path

In the excellent name of my Lord Jesus Christ of Nazareth, the light of the world. You have promised me as You are the light of the world that I will succeed in all that I do and Your light will shine on my path (Job 22:28). I thank You Lord for this statement of blessing. I receive it in Jesus's mighty name. My Lord, how sweet is the taste of Your instructions—sweeter even than honey (Ps. 119:103). Feeling the effect of Your law means more to me than all the money in the world (Ps. 119:72). I thank You, Lord, for Your blessings on me, as I am not a candidate for failure in this world, and none of my descendants will be a candidate for failure. I thank You Lord. *In Jesus's mighty name, amen.*

I Am Trusted

In the trustworthy name of my Lord Jesus Christ of Nazareth.
Father in heaven, when anybody attempts to destroy me
before You, You will throw him out, as You are confident
in my righteousness before You. Lord, You asked Satan,
"Have you considered my servant Job? that there is none
like him on the earth, a blameless and upright man, one
who fears God and shuns evil" (Job 1:8). Lord, when You
bless somebody like myself, that person must continue to
be righteous before You and take Your word as food, as
Job had been doing all the time. Your manifold blessings
will always be part of me, as You have done to me. *In
Jesus's name, amen.*

Patience in the Lord
Results in Blessing

In the holy name of my Lord Jesus Christ of Nazareth. Lord, I know from Your word that the testing of my faith in You produces patience and that patience enables You to know me better as Your faithful child who has been blessed from generation to generation. Your word assures me that I should let my patience have "its perfect work, that I may be perfect and complete lacking nothing" (Jas. 1:4). Lord, the patient father who does things slowly but surely and securely, I sincerely thank You for Your manifold blessings on me and I believe as Your word says that my blessings will be from my generation to generation and thus endless. Thank You, Lord. *In Jesus's name, amen.*

Praying for My Enemies Produces Blessings

In the wonderful name of my Lord Jesus Christ of Nazareth. My father in heaven, Your word builds my spirit daily. I know from Your word that I should bless those who curse me and pray for those who spitefully use me. This is one of the cardinal rules in Your kingdom. I bless anybody who curses me in Jesus's name (Luke 6:28). I do not harbour ill will against anybody in my heart, and neither do I hate anybody in my life. Lord of wonders, as I stand before You, if there is anybody who harbours greed, avarice, and any vice against me, I forgive that person in Jesus's name. Lord, bless that person as You have blessed me. *In Jesus's mighty name, amen.*

Graces of the Heirs of Grace

In the gracious name of my Lord Jesus Christ of Nazareth. As I live by Your grace, You always remind me by Your word to live and hope for every good work You have planned and designed for me as Your word says in Jeremiah 29:11, "For I know the thoughts that I think towards you, Says the Lord, thoughts of Peace and not of evil, to give You a future and a hope." Lord, thank You for thinking peace towards me, which in itself is a blessing to me. *Amen.*

The Loving is Blessed

In the loving name of my Lord Jesus Christ of Nazareth. Your word teaches me to be loving even to my enemy. Lord, You are a father of love. I must follow Your word on love because if I have no love, I am nothing (2 Cor. 13:2). Once I am loving, it is a blessing to me. Lord, build me with Your Spirit of love so that I will continue to be loving to everybody. *In Jesus's mighty name, amen.*

The Blessed Hope

In the glorious name of my Lord Jesus Christ of Nazareth. Your word teaches me that every believer like myself must look for the blessed hope and glorious appearance of our great God and Saviour Jesus Christ, to bless me and my brothers and sisters in Christ. I pray to You Lord to redeem me from evil and purify me and my family for Your good work, which You have destined for us. *In Jesus's mighty name, amen.*

My Blessed Tongue

In the blessed name of my Lord Jesus Christ of Nazareth. Father in heaven, You created me with various parts to my body. Each part has a special function to please You and for the purpose of my creation. You created me to use my tongue to sing songs of praise to praise You, as the whole of Your created beings sang songs of praise to praise You (Ps. 148). Instead of praising You and others with my tongue, I use it to curse men who have been created by You (Jas. 3:9), like myself. Lord God Almighty, in order to obtain the full blessings You have destined for me, forgive me for this attitude of sinfulness in my life and condition my tongue as that of my Lord Jesus Christ who, when the Pharisees and Sadducees tempted Him, controlled His tongue. Lord, control my tongue. *In Jesus's name, amen.*

I Will Be Blessed
on My Deathbed

In the mighty name of my Lord Jesus Christ of Nazareth. My blessing is from generation to generation (Gen. 25:5, 26:12). Your word teaches me that blessed are those who die in the Lord (Rev. 14:13). Lord, protect and guide me on all my ways so that I will die in You in order for my soul to enjoy Your blessings as You have planned for me. *In Jesus's name, amen.*

My Blessing Will Enable Me to Possess the Enemy's Gate

In the powerful name of my Lord Jesus Christ of Nazareth. My heavenly father, You are my only father, who blesses His children, including me. You have assured me in Genesis 22:17 that "Blessing I will bless you, and multiplying I will multiply your descendants as the stars of the heaven, and as the sand which is on the sea shore; and Your descendants shall possess the gate of their enemies." Lord, multiply my descendants as the stars of the heavens and the sand on the seashore, and arm my descendants to capture the gates of their enemies. *In Jesus's name, amen.*

My Blessing Is Everywhere

In the mighty name of my Lord Jesus Christ of Nazareth. My heavenly father, Your word says that I am blessed either in the city or in the country (Deut. 28:3), and blessed shall be the fruit of my body, the produce of my ground and increase of my livestock. I am blessed when I go out or when I come in, because God is with me all the time. Nobody can be against me in Jesus's name. I will see the defeat of my enemies, as the word of my father says: "The Lord will cause your enemies who rise against you to be defeated before your face; they shall come out against you one way and flee before you seven ways" (Deut. 28:7). Anybody professing to be my enemy must be ashamed of himself, because by the nature of God's blessing on me, I become unconquerable. *In Jesus's name, amen.*

God Has Made Me Great

In the mighty name of my Lord Jesus Christ of Nazareth. Merciful father who thinks about all his children, father of all great men and women in Your kingdom, You have promised to make my name great (Gen. 12:2). You are a father who does not change his word. Lord, I receive Your blessings to make my name [your name here] great. *In Jesus's mighty name, amen.*

I Am Rich Because of the Lord's Blessing

In the blessed name of my Lord Jesus Christ of Nazareth. My loving father in heaven, Your word says that "The blessing of the Lord makes one rich. And He adds no sorrow with it" (Prov. 10:22). Lord, thank You for Your blessings that have made me rich in health, finance, business, and family matters. Your blessings to me have made me exceptional to all my colleagues. Lord, continue to drop on me Your showers of blessings. *In Jesus's name, amen.*

God Saves to Be a Blessing

In the gracious name of my Lord Jesus Christ of Nazareth. Salvation belongs to You. When You forgive me my sins and save me from destruction, Your word says that I shall be a blessing (Zech. 8:13) before You. Lord, thank You for exercising Your grace on me. *In Jesus's name, amen.*

Blessing to All the Gentiles

In the wonderful working name of my Lord Jesus Christ of Nazareth. Heavenly father, Your blessing extended from the Jews to the Gentiles, as it is written in Galatians 3:14, saying "that the blessing of Abraham might come upon the Gentiles in Christ Jesus, that we might receive the promise of the Spirit through faith." Lord, as Your word extended to the rest of the whole world (i.e. the Gentiles) through You, I am also blessed, as I am a Gentile. This is through my inheritance as a great-great-grandson of Abraham. *In Jesus's name, amen.*

Bless Me Before I Leave You This Hour

In the blessed name of my Lord Jesus Christ of Nazareth. My heavenly father, as I am already Your blessed son, I will not leave You this hour unless You add extra blessing on me as Jacob demanded from You in Genesis 32:26, saying, "I will not let you go unless you bless me." Lord, just as You added extra blessings to Jacob and changed his name to Israel, I pray before You that You change my name spiritually as You did for Jacob by renaming him Israel. *Amen.*

Thank God

Lord God Almighty, I thank you for listening to my prayers on blessing. I know You have blessed me, but I must ask for more blessings. *In Jesus's name, amen.*

Grace

The grace of my Lord Jesus Christ, the love of God, and the fellowship of the Holy Spirit be with me now and forever more. *Amen.* Surely good angels of God and their mercies are following me with all my blessings all the days of my life as I dwell in the house of my Lord forever and ever. *In Jesus's mighty name, amen.*

Printed in the United States
By Bookmasters